| | DATE DUE | | |
|---|---|---|---|
| | | | |
| | | | |
| | | | |
| | | | |
| | | | |
| | | | |
| | | | |
| | | | |
| | | | |
| | | | |

CUTTING-EDGE CAREERS™

# CAREERS IN
# ARTIFICIAL
# INTELLIGENCE

Robert Greenberger

ROSEN
PUBLISHING®

New York

*To the Malibu gang, notably TYG, without whose help*
*this book would not have been possible*

Published in 2007 by The Rosen Publishing Group, Inc.
29 East 21st Street, New York, NY 10010

**Library of Congress Cataloging-in-Publication Data**

Greenberger, Robert.
Careers in artificial intelligence/Robert Greenberger.—1st ed.
    p. cm.—(Cutting-edge careers)
Includes bibliographical references and index.
ISBN-13: 978-1-4042-0953-4
ISBN-10: 1-4042-0953-0 (library binding)
1. Artificial intelligence—Vocational guidance. I. Title. II. Series.
Q335.G744 2006
006.3023—dc22

                                                    2006016957

*Manufactured in the United States of America*

# CONTENTS

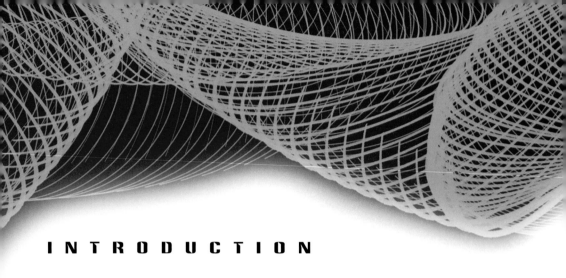

# INTRODUCTION

**[S]** ometimes without realizing it, people are exposed to artificial intelligence (AI), which is the ability of computers to mimic humanlike thought processes. Now more than ever before, computers employ various forms of AI in the home, in school, and at work. Some basic examples of AI might include the movie suggestions from your digital video recorder based on your previous programming choices, or your microwave knowing when your popcorn is ready, or video game software with realistic and lifelike oncoming traffic. All of these activities, and countless others, are possible because of sophisticated programs that mimic human responses.

Artificial intelligence is a field that is just half a century old, but it is growing rapidly. Corporations, laboratories, and universities around the world are trying to develop AI programming to simplify tasks or aid human development, rapidly changing the world in which we live and interact.

In July 2006, a *New York Times* reporter wrote, "The advances can be seen in the emergence of bold new projects intended to create more ambitious machines that can improve safety and security, entertain and inform, or just handle everyday tasks. At Stanford University, for instance, computer scientists are developing a robot that can use a hammer and screwdriver to assemble an Ikea bookcase (a project

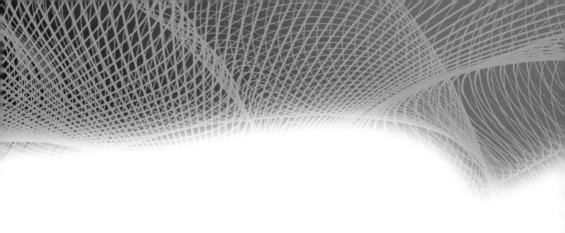

beyond the reach of many humans) as well as tidy up after a party, load a dishwasher, or take out the trash."

As computers process information faster and the physical limitations of computers shrink, the ability to create new devices or operating systems increases. As a result, the careers that revolve around software development and computer programming are growing at a tremendous pace. Degree programs that are geared toward careers in computer technology are also increasing to keep up with this demand. Ultimately, this shift will prepare a new generation to enter commercial or research applications. Of these technology careers, AI may be among the most cutting-edge choices because new AI applications are constantly being developed.

# CHAPTER 1

# A History of Artificial Intelligence

In 1956, a group of scientists and computer engineers met at Dartmouth College to better understand where their collective research into a specific style of computing was headed. While there, John McCarthy of the mathematics department called the branch "artificial intelligence," and the name stuck.

"At the 1956 Dartmouth Artificial Intelligence Conference, an audacious, outrageous even, intellectual Zeitgeist emerged: that the core of humanity, our ability to think and reason, was subject to our own technological understanding, a recursive formulation of our very nature. And the participants were right," said Rodney Brooks, the Panasonic Professor of Robotics and director of the Massachusetts Institute of Technology (MIT) Computer Science and Artificial Intelligence Lab.

J. Presper Eckert *(left)* and John W. Mauchly are pictured with the Electronic Numerical Integrator and Computer (ENIAC), the precursor to the personal computer, in this University of Pennsylvania photo.

Earlier computers were merely devices to perform mathematical tasks. The history of AI and computers can be traced back 5,000 years to Asia and the development of the abacus. This device, still in use in parts of the world today, developed the principals in calculating numbers that also formed the first computer programs.

It wasn't until 1642, however, that Blaise Pascal invented the world's first automatic calculating machine, called the Pascaline. From this humble beginning, people spent the next several centuries trying to

The English mathematician Charles Babbage worked on the differential calculating machine, shown here in part, for 37 years, prior to it being rejected for
an English patent in 1842.

find ways to have computers do more complex calculations. Some milestone inventions on the path to today's supercomputers include Gottfried Wilhelm von Leibniz's 1694 Leibniz computer, noteworthy for its use of algorithms, a concept still employed by today's devices.

In 1805, Joseph-Marie Jacquard devised a method for automated weaving that is seen as a precursor to early computer technology. The weaving looms were directed by instructions on a series of punched cards, like computers would be instructed later.

Charles Babbage wrote *Observations on the Application of Machinery to the Computation of Mathematical Tables*, earning him the British Astronomical Society's first gold medal in 1821. Babbage built his difference engine a year later but abandoned it as unwieldy. He imagined building a machine that would perform calculations and was aided by Ada Lovelace, Lord Byron's child, who came up with programming ideas, hence making her the first software engineer. She wrote in 1843 of how the analytical engine could be employed to play chess or compose music.

Herman Hollerith built upon the advancements made throughout the nineteenth century and patented an electromechanical information device that used punched cards. It won the 1890 U.S. Census competition, thus introducing the use of electricity in a major data-processing project. Hollerith founded the Tabulating Machine Company in 1896, which eventually evolved into International Business Machines, or IBM.

In 1940, Alan Turing led a group of mathematicians and electrical engineers in finding a way to crack Germany's military codes during World War II. They used telephone relays and other electromagnetic pieces to construct Robinson, the first computer. As Adolf Hitler's men added more complex codes through their Enigma machine, the Allied team kept pace, replacing Robinson with Colossus in 1943, using 2,000 radio vacuum tubes. Colossus and nine similar computers worked throughout WW II to counter the German offensive.

This version of a 1960s IBM computer system required frequent monitoring. By the 1980s, IBM became the first American company to manufacture the personal computer, which is today considered invaluable.

In 1941, Konrad Zue developed the world's first fully programmable digital computer, the Z-3. Arnold Fast, a blind mathematician, was hired to program the Z-3, making him the first working programmer. After this point, the development of computing machines sped up

with names like the Mark I, ENIAC, and UNIVAC, but they all were huge, slow-processing machines dependent on vacuum tubes.

William Bradford Shockley, Walter Hauser Brittain, and John Bardeen invented the transistor in 1947, which revolutionized electronic devices in general. As computer speed improved, the hardware began to shrink also, as transistors took up less space than the older vacuum tubes.

David Weil, curator of the Computer Museum of America, located in San Diego, California, is seen behind a showcase of vacuum tubes and other computer parts from the 1950s.

## Teaching Intelligence

Alan Turing continued his research, believing computers could do more than calculate numbers. In 1950 he wrote a paper, "Computing Machinery and Intelligence," which truly began the branch of computer science known today as AI. With David Campernowne, Turing wrote the first program allowing a computer to play chess against a human. Given the rules of chess, it became the standard against which machine intelligence was measured. Additionally, Turing developed

## MARVIN MINSKY

Marvin Lee Minsky (1927– ) has been one of the leading developers of artificial intelligence since the 1950s, when the term was coined. He cofounded MIT's AI Laboratory, but is best known for his written works on AI and its philosophical implications.

Minsky was said to be a prodigy in both math and music. In high school, he focused on intelligence, going on to study mathematics at Harvard (1950) and Princeton (1954). Restless, he sought inspiration and enlightenment from other disciplines as he tried to understand how the mind worked.

With a colleague in 1951, Minsky built a machine named SNARC that could master maneuvering through a maze. This is considered the construction of the first neural network that prompted his doctoral thesis on automated learning.

Since then, Minsky has worked exclusively with computers, attending the Dartmouth conference where the term "artificial intelligence" was introduced. With John McCarthy, he founded MIT's AI Lab in 1959, where he remains today. Minsky has made a career out of studying the brain, intelligence, and

*Marvin Minsky has made lifelong contributions to the science of artificial intelligence and robotics, and wrote one of the premier books on AI,* The Society of Mind.

*(continued on following page)*

(continued from previous page)

learning, applying much of that information to designing computer systems that can learn. He considers himself the living authority on the human mind.

Minsky's achievements have been rewarded with numerous patents, including the development of the first graphics display visible from a head-mounted device in 1963. He also consulted with director Stanley Kubrick on how AI should be employed in the film *2001: A Space Odyssey*. Minsky has been honored around the world for his efforts.

another challenge, now known as the Turing test. This called for a human to use a computer terminal to interact in conversations with several different people, as well as with the machine. If the human could not determine which of the conversations were with a person and which were with the machine, the test had been passed and the machine would be considered "intelligent." The annual Loebner Contest was held at Rutgers University in New Jersey with a $100,000 reward for the machine that could pass the test.

In the 1960s, Daniel G. Bobrow wrote a program called Student that could solve algebra problems from English-language stories. Thomas G. Evans repeated that success with his own program, Analogy. Edward A. Feigenbaum wrote the program DENDRAL, which performed simple calculations necessary for the study of chemistry.

People began predicting the limitless horizon for computer programming, suspecting machines would soon compose music, translate languages, and play chess at the grandmaster level. Those predictions eventually came to pass, but achieving them took much longer than expected.

The field of AI earned its place in the public consciousness with the rise of video games, first in arcades in the 1970s and then, starting in the 1980s, with handheld devices and home game platforms such as Atari and Intellivision.

It wasn't until the late 1990s, however, that some of the early predictions about AI came to pass. Deep Blue, a supercomputer, defeated chess master Gary Kasparov in successive matches in 1997. Since then, other countries have used chess as a benchmark for their own AI program developments, including a summer 2006 competition in China.

# CHAPTER 2

# Practical Applications of Artificial Intelligence

While scientists, engineers, and computer programmers were excited at the development of artificial intelligence throughout the 1950s, other applications were slow to be employed until the military discovered practical uses for AI. The Defense Advanced Research Projects Agency (DARPA) was founded in 1958 as a response to the Soviet Union launching the first artificial satellite, *Sputnik*. The mission of DARPA was to anticipate applications for AI, considering what the military leaders of tomorrow might need to be more effective. After the Gulf War of the 1990s, DARPA said that using AI to schedule military units in the Middle East more than justified all U.S. military spending since 1958. In that time, the military has employed AI to identify enemy aircraft and weapons, and target distant objects.

Dr. Melissa Holland *(left)*, Calandra Tate *(center)*, and Dr. Clare Voss each hold portable language translators that rely upon AI technology and are in use by U.S. troops in Iraq.

The use of autopilot technology on airplanes is one of the earliest uses of AI in the civilian world. Developed by Sperry Corporation, the autopilot took control of the hydraulically operated rudder, elevator, and ailerons, allowing aircraft to fly straight without a pilot's touch. These tasks accounted for up to 80 percent of a pilot's flight time and allowed pilots to take periodic breaks from flying, leading to a dramatic reduction in pilot error. Today's autopilots now help control the take-off, ascent, level, approach, and landing of airplanes.

During the 1970s, AI began being used to scan and recognize the printed word and synthesize a voice, allowing machines to read to the blind. Similar scanning technology allows the printed page to be turned into digital files for electronic publishing and archiving. A related field has allowed for voice recognition programming to

## ARTIFICIAL INTELLIGENCE IN MEDIA

As scientists searched for ways to make machines calculate and then think, writers kept pace. One could argue that Mary Wollstonecraft Shelley's *Frankenstein* featured the first use of AI, since the creature had a brain transplanted into its body. The first noteworthy fictional piece about AI was by Karel Capek, who coined the term "robot" in his 1921 drama, *R.U.R. (Rossum's Universal Robots)*. The play postulated intelligent machines, built as servants, which subsequently rebelled and destroyed their makers.

As computing devices continued to develop, the potential for AI to be a center point for fictional stories grew. George Orwell envisioned a bleak future under computer control in his classic dystopia, *1984*. Another story of AI run amok is the Arthur C. Clarke and Stanley Kubrick collaboration, *2001: A Space Odyssey*.

*Daniel A. Reed, Computer Science Department head at the University of Illinois, sits behind Illiac computers, the inspiration for HAL, the "thinking" computer of the film* 2001: A Space Odyssey.

Fritz Lang's silent film *Metropolis* featured one of the first notable robots in a sympathetic light. Since then, artificial life-forms have populated novels, plays, movies, television programs, and comic books. In the *Star Wars* saga, all such mechanical devices are nicknamed "droids," although R2-D2 is a robot. *Star Trek: The Next Generation's* Data is a perfect example of an android. More recently, Steven Spielberg directed *AI*, a film about a world of androids, including a young boy model played by Haley Joel Osment. The somber production showed how these constructs formed their own culture and society.

translate the spoken word into a computer-generated written word. People with disabilities have benefited greatly from AI, which is also used to control wheelchairs and other devices.

The medical world has taken full advantage of AI to help improve patient diagnosis. For instance, neural networks (interconnected groups of artificial neurons) are used to assist doctors in finding patterns and relationships in data. In a study conducted by Lars Edenbrandt, M.D., Ph.D., and coauthor Bo Heden, M.D., Ph.D., of the University Hospital in Lund, Sweden, neural networks can more accurately read electrocardiograms than ever before. Cardiologists interpret these tests, normally used on heart attack patients, to help them determine the best course of treatment. "The neural networks performed higher than an experienced cardiologist, indicating that they may be useful as decision support," Edenbrandt told the American Heart Association. To conduct the test, the computer program was

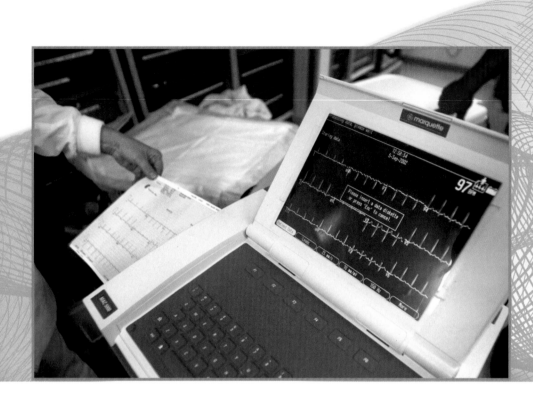

A nurse at a New York hospital uses computer technology to record patient data. More and more, medical professionals are relying upon technology to help record and interpret test results.

loaded with thousands of electrocardiogram readings so it could determine when a patient was suffering a heart attack.

Hearing aids have also improved thanks to AI, as reported at the 2006 Canadian Hard of Hearing Association meeting. Karla Rissling of the Medicine Hat Hearing Centre reported that AI can optimize speech-specific user preferences such as differentiating between loud or quiet environments.

AI is now being employed to create more lifelike prosthetics. The *Los Angeles Times* noted in 2006, "One knee . . . will even mimic lost muscle activity by powering ankle and leg amputees up stairs, or up from a sitting position. But that's just the beginning. Advances in

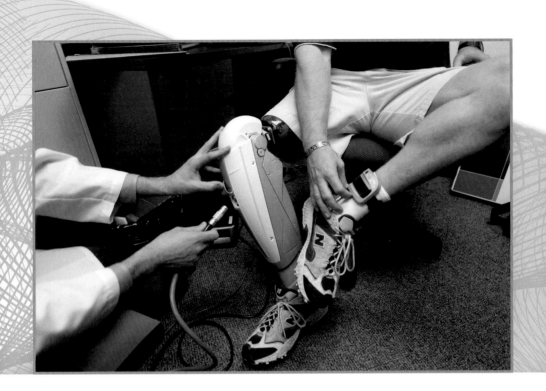

Retired U.S. Army Ranger Bill Dunham makes an adjustment on the Power Knee, the first prosthetic leg with artificial intelligence, on March 30, 2006, in New York.

robotics, electronics and tissue engineering ultimately could create ways to lengthen damaged limbs, grow new cartilage, skin and bone, and permanently affix a prosthetic device to the body. Some researchers are even designing a so-called biohybrid limb—a prosthesis that can be controlled by the user's thoughts." Work just like this is now being accomplished at Cyberkinetics Neurotechnology Systems, Inc., where they are developing a system called BrainGate. The software will decode brain waves via a small chip in the brain's primary motor cortex, turning them into computer commands.

Announcements are constantly being made regarding new products and services that use AI, which means that associated career opportunities are particularly bright. Dr. Anthony Francis of Google notes, "There are so many areas of AI—military applications (general planning and education), information retrieval (search and data mining), game AI (believable characters), theoretical research (cool algorithms), robotics (even cooler whirring gears and der blinkenlights—the modern term for the diagnostic lights of mainframe computers), simulation (crowds, traffic, etc.), and cognitive science (models of mind and the human connection)."

# CHAPTER 3

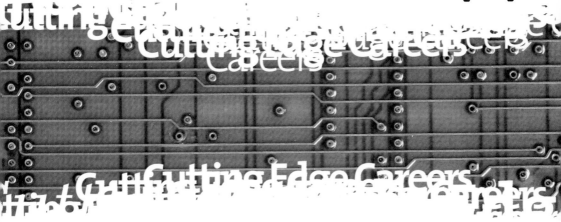

# Artificial Intelligence and the Job Market

If the applications of artificial intelligence fascinate you, then you might want to consider working in this diverse field. But what do you do to prepare for a future career in AI? According to the American Association for Artificial Intelligence (AAAI), "There are many types of jobs and careers involving AI, but two of the usual dichotomies are: academic vs. industrial jobs, and research vs. application jobs." In all cases, a solid preparation in the tools of the trade is recommended, including programming languages, algorithm design, operating systems, data structures, logic and mathematics, probability theory and statistics, and the specialized topics covered in AI courses. These subjects are standard courses in most undergraduate and graduate computer science programs.

Sophisticated computer games like *Sid Meier's Civilization III: Complete* use artificial intelligence to anticipate player response, making the gaming experience more challenging.

But understanding AI requires more than computer programming abilities. In fact, the AAAI states that many careers in AI, especially those in an academic or industrial setting, will likely require more advanced degrees beyond a BS or BA. In some cases, on-the-job training that helps to explain instructional systems and basic robotics might help a person become more competitive in the field of AI.

Video and computer games currently remain one of the most popular applications of AI. In order to create games with characters that "think" like humans do, programmers work with AI technology to simulate our world. The first effective use of AI in computer gaming was used in first-person combat games such as *Doom*. Neural networks, like those discussed in chapter 2, evolved to heightening a game's degree of difficulty. The network, imitating the human brain, gauges the player's tactics and responds to counter them, thus creating new challenges. Games such as *The Sims* and *Civilization* have been built from neural networks.

In a survey at the 1999 Game Developers Conference, 60 percent of the attendees at a roundtable meeting reported their projects included one or more dedicated AI programmers, up from 46 percent in 1998, and 24 percent in 1997. These percentages are only expected to increase in the future.

At the 2006 Game Developers Conference, there was as much discussion over the technical side of creating games. Topics included complex data mapping production techniques in 3-D, advanced light and shadow culling methods, and present and future techniques in AI.

# Lead Game Designer

Geoffrey "GZ" Zatkin, cofounder and chief operating officer (COO) of XSG, a startup company working in the games industry, took his passion for gaming and turned it into a career. Zatkin went from playing fantasy games such as *Dungeons & Dragons, Cyberpunk, Car Wars,* and *Magic: The Gathering* to creating them. He often bought games just for the chance to deconstruct them. When Zatkin was in college, he was playing and programming MUDs (text-based multiplayer games) that were the precursors to the multiplayer (MMO) games that are now popular. "I started in 1997 as a level designer for the small team developing the multiplayer game *EverQuest*, at 989 Studios. As the team expanded, I moved from my level design position to be one of the first game designers on the team."

After working on *EverQuest* through its launch, Zatkin worked on *EverQuest*'s sequel game, *EverQuest II*. He was subsequently picked as the senior designer on another MMO game, *Sovereign*, and has since worked for Sony Online Entertainment and Monolith Productions.

An exhibitor demonstrates a computer game at the Entertainment Software Association's 2006 expo in Los Angeles. Game designers increasingly rely upon AI technology to make games more stimulating.

Zatkin described his work as similar to that of the screenwriter for a motion picture. Game designers generate hundreds of pages of documentation, known as the design document, that set the game's guidelines. The design document covers all of the game's aspects, whether they are extremely broad (genre, setting, player goals) or specific (control scheme and logic), and helps control every character's ability.

## Skills and Requirements

According to Zatkin, lead designers need to have prior experience working on a variety of games, as well as effective management skills. If you compare the design of a computer game to a major film, the lead designer is the lead scriptwriter and movie director. In addition to his or her design duties, the lead designer is responsible for assigning tasks, getting the design team to follow a rigid schedule, and seeing the project through according to the constraints of time and the budget. Lead designers also work with designers from other departments, including art, engineering, management, and testing. This work usually involves explaining key game concepts, receiving feedback on the design, and scheduling. The lead designer is responsible for making sure that his or her entire team is operating efficiently and that all departments have the information they need.

AI is found in just about every video game available across all platforms. It is used commonly in pathfinding, which is the ability of AI entities, non-player characters (NPCs), to successfully navigate their way through the game world. Zatkin said, "Oftentimes, this is not just a single entity moving, and in extreme cases, can involve hundreds or thousands of AI entities moving in formations over extremely complicated virtual terrain. Depending upon the type of game, [AI] could [influence] anything from enemy soldiers, race cars, a self-guided missile seeking its target, or a football wide receiver trying to outrun your avatar to the football."

AI is written into the computer programs for most of today's games. For example, in a racing game, AI controls the other cars, while in a combat or sports game, AI controls the opponents' tactical decisions, directing them to move, shoot, or jump. In a strategy game, AI controls the enemies, manages their resources, and decides when they should attack.

Zatkin graduated with a bachelor's degree in psychology, but unlike many with AI careers, he has no master's degree. "Psychology was a good major for me," he said, "because psychology is about understanding how people think and how/why they behave as they do in certain circumstances. This is surprisingly relevant to video game design."

For those wishing to follow in Zatkin's footsteps, he stressed that a designer working in AI will need to possess strong logic skills. Being able to program in languages such as C and C++ is a major requirement. "As an AI engineer, a computer science degree is very handy, as are courses in cognitive psychology. Many programmers in the games industry are more interested in your skill and past experience than where you went to school. That being said, if you don't have an impressive résumé to back you up, a degree is a very good starting point."

He did note, though, that the video game design field is surprisingly narrow. As a result, when people wish to move and can't find another company, they drift into other fields. Engineers and computer artists have a much easier time finding non-video game work, as there is almost always a demand for highly trained people who know how to program or produce computer art. For beginning designers, Zatkin added, annual salaries can start at $25,000, with experienced designers topping out in excess of $100,000. The average salary is in the $40,000–$65,000 range. "However," Zatkin warned, "don't go into video games for the money. Most game industry people work extremely long hours in very stressful environments."

As new generations of hardware with more processing power become less expensive, the use of AI in video gaming will become even more realistic. With that in mind, Zatkin urged prospective designers to study their craft. "Quite often, the games industry is a meritocracy. Those with superior skill are more highly acknowledged than those without. One of the hardest parts of getting into the games industry is actually getting in. Once you have worked on a game or two, moving between companies is easy and commonly done." As for final advice, Zatkin urged teenagers who are interested in AI to build demos and mods (modifications of games), learn the computer language Java, and have the ability to show your work in source code.

## Engineer

When you use a search engine, typing in key words results in instantaneous results, but refining those results and providing the user with more accurate information is the task of many engineers, including Google's Dr. Anthony Francis. "My official title on my business cards is Renaissance Engineer – Search Quality. If you want something less prosaic, then I'm a member of the technical staff, or in Googlespeak, simply an Engineer," he said.

Dr. Francis described his current role as "making a computer's memory better based on context." He builds systems that try to understand how people search the Internet so that their results reflect the most relevant information. He became interested in AI through his interest in science fiction, including the robot stories of Isaac Asimov, the computers on *Star Trek*, and Hal 9000 from *2001*. However, it wasn't until college that he decided to make a career out of his interests in AI.

One area Dr. Francis concentrated on is contextual information retrieval. He described it as, "Humans can remember an amazing amount of information and yet we are not distracted by all the other things that we know. If I'm talking to you about *Star Wars* and say 'Ford,' you'll think of Harrison Ford, but if we were talking about Mustangs, you would think of Ford Motor Company without skipping a beat. My goal was to make computers do the same thing."

Dr. Francis explained various AI applications and how they are achieved, including "design intelligence," which is done by studying the algorithms of how a human or animal responds and then tailoring computer programs to replicate those responses. This study of algorithms is called cognitive science, an entire field of AI that has produced very interesting results. Understanding algorithms is important because it allows engineers to attempt to predict human behavior and responses. This idea, according to Dr. Francis, is where design intelligence becomes AI.

"But [design intelligence] only goes so far. As computer problems get larger and more complex, the task of studying algorithms becomes too difficult." This is where "machine learning," or exposing a computer to evidence and letting it come up with its own answers, is applied. The difficult aspect of machine learning is that computers cannot work on their own—a human must first determine relevant questions and build a framework for capturing predictable answers. Dr. Francis offered an example of how machine learning is used for AI. "The robot pet I worked on at Yamaha is a good example," he said. "The engineers who built it gave it a half dozen senses, but to make it learn who liked it we had to teach it to recognize people by sight and to interpret a touch on the head as a friendly pat. Then the pet behaved in a 'natural' way. That's machine learning and design intelligence working together. Machine learning is huge at Google, and at any large company that has to analyze a lot of data, a process called data mining."

Another area of AI revolves around designing machines that can make choices. The military uses AI planning and logistics by providing

This tiny hearing aid made by Oticon uses artificial intelligence and a microprocessor to detect and distinguish sounds while filtering out distractions.

computers with details and then using those same computers to help determine complicated plans to move heavy equipment and troops in an effective way.

As for preparing for a career, Dr. Francis explained that a background in computer science is important, but understanding the common programming languages can be even more useful. "Computer languages are constantly in flux," he said. "One of the first computer languages used for AI (indeed, one of the first computer languages in wide use) is Lisp. Lisp stands for LISt Processing and focuses on giving a computer programmer powerful tools to manipulate symbols. Lisp is still in use, and many hardcore programmers argue that you need to know it to understand the techniques it used. It's very, very easy to do complicated AI algorithms in Lisp. However, it is a specialized language and you need to know a mainstream language as well."

# Engineer Director

In 2005, Dr. Daniel Clancy left a career in the National Aeronautics and Space Administration (NASA), joining Google as engineer director for Google Book Search. He explained, "When I began studying, I thought about things like AI and parallel programming but chose AI because it lends itself to different disciplines, including cognitive science, computers, and even philosophy. AI attracted me because it was asking some interesting questions about intelligence." Dr. Clancy received his Ph.D. at the University of Texas at Austin in 1997 and then sought a job in research. After some deliberation, he selected a position at NASA.

"When I joined, NASA was rebuilding their AI capabilities . . . I joined NASA during their remote agent experiment, the first sort of AI-appliance-based software that received a fair amount of notoriety. We put a team together to build the software architecture for the *Cassini* orbital insertion. In most space flights, there's a detailed command sequence, but if the environment behaves differently than expected, the command sequence could break. You'd need to start over again, which was problematic for robotic missions."

Based on his success with *Cassini*, Dr. Clancy and his team went to work on *Deep Space One*, an experimental satellite. In addition to the AI technology to direct the satellite, it contained nine other experiments. "The idea was to give the spacecraft high-level goals," Dr. Clancy said, "[and use AI to] let the spacecraft figure out for itself how to accomplish those goals, when to do [them], and [how to] maximize resources. System Health Management (SHM) was a [program] that included monitoring the spacecraft, finding a problem, and understanding how to handle recovery action."

The National Aeronautics and Space Administration (NASA) continually employs the use of AI technology, like with this Field Integrated Design and Operations (FIDO) rover that simulates the conditions on Mars.

Soon after joining NASA, Dr. Clancy recognized he had a set of skills that extended beyond research, so he began seeking a role in management. "As opposed to being the person sitting there writing the code and figuring out algorithms, the contribution that most distinguished myself was [both my] technical skills [and] my ability to communicate and manage."

His proposals on further uses of the SHM in the space shuttle led him to become a team leader; eventually he directed the Computer Sciences Division. There, he oversaw the work of more than 300 researchers, most of whom did AI work. Dr. Clancy said one of his biggest accomplishments was getting AI technology included in the Mars Rover mission. "After the mission," he said, "scientists said they yielded 30 percent more information because our software led to greater efficiency aboard the craft."

After seven years with NASA, Dr. Clancy recognized it might be time to move on; he felt he had done all he could within NASA. "I believe all of us are driven by the desire to have an impact in the world, on our lives, with our friends. One reason I went into research was a leveraged impact. My leveraged impact was as much managing and building strong teams [as it was] articulating what needed to be done."

He selected a position at Google because he was driven by the service that the search engine had become. "At its heart, Google's a technology company, not just an Internet company," Dr. Clancy explained. "Given an opportunity, Google would focus on how innovation would solve the problem. For example, Book Search solved a problem. It's an ambitious, long-term endeavor, sort of Google's 'moon' shot, and not the type of thing Internet companies engage in. This is really a five- to ten-year vision; to make the world's printed content searchable online."

When Google began its print initiative, scanning technology proved prohibitively expensive, so it set its researchers to work on developing a new method for scanning. Dr. Clancy arrived after the

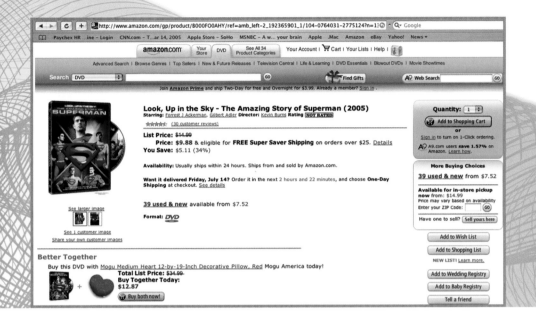

Amazon.com is among the first Web sites that employed the use of artificial intelligence to personalize a shopper's experience by offering him or her related goods based upon past purchases.

new technology had proven itself successful. His job was to develop ways to "scale" the technology to handle larger amounts of print in order to accomplish Google's long-term goal.

## A Career with Options

Dr. Clancy advised students who are interested in AI to look at its full range of possibilities. "Students need to ask themselves if they love AI because they feel it's a set of techniques to solve hard and interesting problems, or if they love AI because they are passionate about the grand vision of a 'thinking' machine. Personally, I view AI and its success as parts of a larger system. AI can be found in some of what we do at Google, but not everything. AI is part of scanning, but not all of it. Certainly AI can be employed in Web search engines, some not. Shopping comparison sites, or the book recommendations from Amazon use AI [to recommend specific media to repeat shoppers]."

Dr. Clancy suggested that students study robotics because "robotics is imbedded in the physical world. When you're starting out in high school, there's real value in having something that is physically embodied in engaging the world. In the past, robotic behavior was limited, now we're getting to the point where you can get fairly sophisticated behavior at a low cost. I think there's real value in not staying abstract, but to physically develop something that lives, behaves, and acts in the world."

# Computer Scientist

Bill Cheetham has been a computer scientist at General Electric for the last twenty years. However, the nature of his work has evolved, as has the technology around him. Cheetham is now a part of GE's Industrial Artificial Intelligence Laboratory, a division of the conglomerate that helps solve problems using technology, including AI.

"I'm usually working on two projects at a time," Cheetham said from his office near Albany, New York. "These can last anywhere from six months to three years."

He described the process using one of his projects involving gas turbine engines that generate electricity for municipalities. His goal was to use AI to diagnose maintenance issues with the turbines, which were studded with 100 sensors that continually generate data.

The first step in the process was creating a team that involved Cheetham, another member of the AI group, four people from the gas turbine manufacturing company, and at least one of the end users from GE's information technology department.

To be more effective, Cheetham took classes in turbine maintenance and spoke at length with mechanics about diagnostic testing. Where

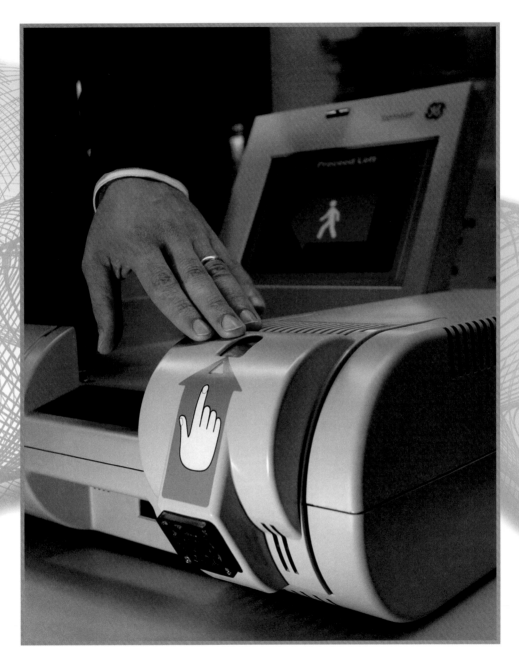

A General Electric representative demonstrates an explosives-detecting finger scanner at the San Francisco International Airport in 2005. The use of AI technology is increasingly beneficial in creating electronics for security.

it was once common to examine and interpret data by hand, pouring the figures into a software program such as Excel and then creating a graph based on the data, Cheetham was now tasked with implementing the use of AI technology to help maintain the engines. During this research process, he visited the manufacturing facility, saw the turbines in use, studied where the sensors were located, and noted the types of data they recorded.

After studying the system, Cheetham began determining how AI could be used to help solve turbine maintenance problems. Much discussion over the design for such a system occurred before any real programming was started. "That wouldn't even be the start of the code. We talk among ourselves to see how to improve [maintenance], then we go in and start coding, then we test the code, then go back to the users. If they like it, we'll expand on it. That's the discipline called software engineering," he explained.

Cheetham's team wrote software with algorithms to sift through the voluminous data to detect flaws and even recommend repairs. His area of expertise is in case-based reasoning—reasoning through experience—using expertise from the past to solve a problem. In some cases, Cheetham said changes in manufacturing might be required that would then be discussed with the engineers. Similar work was done with diagnosing aircraft engines, and he said they pooled data from GE–built airline engines so the database was filled with information from thousands of engines, allowing the computer to find anomalies.

## Education Programs

Cheetham said most major companies have similar divisions that offer college graduates a wide variety of career choices. To prepare for a career in AI, he suggested majoring in computer science, electrical engineering, or mechanical engineering. Students should also master the computer languages C++ and Java. Upon graduation, they should seriously consider getting their master's degree or find a company that would help fund continuing education. Cheetham took advantage of GE's Edison Engineering Program. While working for GE, he was assigned to three different one-year projects while also attending a local university to study for his degree.

While a Ph.D. isn't required, Cheetham noted that 40 percent of his colleagues have at least six years of college education. Students fresh from college could expect to start work in a similar field earning $50,000–$60,000 a year. With each advanced degree, the person's earning power greatly increases, and those with a Ph.D. can also branch out into teaching.

Cheetham sees a bright future for AI in general, but he suggested that the robotics field may be among the leading cutting-edge careers of the future, since robots will soon be found doing everything from household chores to taking part in military conflicts. "A century ago, there was an industrial revolution with mechanical tasks being completed on assembly lines that made the tasks more efficient. Today, most people are doing mental tasks, knowledge-based tasks. AI helps people perform those knowledge-based tasks, and AI technology is striving to automate tasks where possible. AI can interpret data, make a decision, make sure it's right, and then complete a task so no human has to intervene. In the future, repetitive tasks are things computers will do. AI can organize data, making it easier for a person to see, and that makes people more effective."

# CHAPTER 4

# Research and Development of Future AI Technology

American companies are spending more and more time and money on the study of artificial intelligence for future applications. One such company that is paving the way in AI research and development is Microsoft. Eric Horvitz is a principal researcher at Microsoft Research's Adaptive Systems & Interaction Group. Horvitz is also the president of the AI trade group the American Association for Artificial Intelligence (AAAI).

"I'm working at a modern-day Bell Labs, in probably the largest software research company in the world. IBM may be larger, but they're hardware and software; we're just software. About one-quarter of Microsoft's research is AI research," Horvitz said, referring to AT&T's legendary Bell Labs research

Steven Wesley, regional administrator of the Delaware juvenile probation program, holds a global positioning transmitter that tracks the movements of minors who are under house arrest.

division. He explained that AI has grown so diverse that there are subsets of pure research that use AI in some way. Horvitz estimated that among the 800 researchers employed by Microsoft around the world—in places like Cambridge, Massachusetts; California's Silicon Valley region; Beijing, China; Bangalore, India; and the company's Redmond, Washington, headquarters—about one-quarter of the work done involves AI. Some of those groups include the Natural Language Processing Research Team, the Adaptive Systems Research Team, the Speech Research Team, and the Vision Research Team.

Horvitz is part of Microsoft's Adaptive Systems and Interaction Team. Every day he handles a broad range of research on topics that deal with integrating technology with software to make services more adaptive. One such system uses satellites to help people reach their destinations. Horvitz explained, "For the last two years, we've provided volunteers with fifty global positioning systems, for two weeks each, to use as they drove around Seattle. We then amassed data on hundreds of trips in Seattle, so we've created something called Pre-Destination. The idea is to predict where they are driving just as soon as they start moving their car. With that knowledge, we can layer in a number of services for their dashboard screen such as directions, advertising, and other opportunistic placements. We also have something called Shortstop where we can predict how long a stop will be based on stored criteria that can be applied in a smart way. We can determine, based on the length of the stop, whether or not there's time to deliver messages."

## Anticipating Consumer Needs

Horvitz explained that Microsoft is working on numerous ways to study data and human behavior in order to have computer programs become more tailored to meet an individual's needs. Many of these new software AI applications have evolved out of the mobile workforce, with people no longer working solely at a desk inside an office. Employees now keep in touch with supervisors or family members through mobile devices ranging from cell phones and laptop computers to wireless personal digital assistants (PDAs). The AI teams at Microsoft are developing applications to make those systems communicate and function more efficiently.

"We're building large infrastructures that present a vision of how communications will work some day," Horvitz said. "There will be software agents that will deliver new ways for callers to communicate. We're calling it Bestcom, which is determining the most efficient way to get in contact with the software agent working on people's

Microsoft's Eric Horvitz holds a "smart" phone that uses AI technology and global positioning software to allow users to predict traffic buildup before getting held up in bumper-to-bumper snarls.

behalf. It's similar to something [else] we're building called Smart Secretary.

"There will be systems that balance the context of users against the balance of costs for disruption of messages coming in, versus the benefits of allowing them through. There will be a system that can look at your calendar and your desktop activity, using cameras and microphones, to assign a level of interruptability to people. Right now, I use the Busybuddy system, which will see how busy I am and hold messages and calls.

"From there, we built a system to evaluate how important messages are. It's called the Priorities System. It assigns e-mail and measures the cost of delayed review and assigns each message a number from 0–100. We'll then capture a notion of each message's urgency and the system will 'learn' that by watching a person work with his or her e-mail. The Priorities System will learn to only alert a person, [anticipate] when he or she is busy, and then deliver important messages [as needed]. We hope to have a system determine when we're away from the desk when to send an e-mail or message to a cell phone or PDA. The changes in computing mean we're building elegant tools that work on your behalf while keeping you informed and letting you work."

At Microsoft, the majority of employees have advanced degrees. However, as the various research labs at Microsoft and other firms such as Yahoo!, Google, IBM, ATT, GE, and NEC grow, people fresh out of college with an undergraduate degree will be able to find entry-level work. These positions include program managers, software developers, and information architects. "Undergrads should have a background to the side of their core work in psychology, and it's always good to take one philosophy of the mind class to understand the mind at a fundamental level," Horvitz said. "It's always great to have some biology background to understand nervous systems to keep people broadminded about human intelligence. They should [also] take a good dose of mathematics and computer science curriculum. Math should include a logic class and a good class on probability theory."

# Academics

An overlooked career in AI is based around teaching the concepts and applications of AI through ongoing research that may prove fruitful as the technology improves.

In the spring of 2006, three students at India's Jaipur-based Global Institute of Technology built something they named the Artificial Intelligence Military Support System. The goal was to provide better border security in the Rajasthan region by creating a web of lasers to detect movement across the border and then have the computer determine the level of threat and the appropriate response. It worked well enough for India's military to study its long-term applications.

Atlanta-born professor Jim Davies chose the academic route to a career in AI. He teaches at Carleton University's Institute of Cognitive Science. "Cognitive science is kind of like physics was before Newton," Davies explained. "We know so little about it; it's a field that's very important, very interesting to me. There could be major science revolutions in my lifetime, and there's a chance to be a part of one. I liked the different, interdisciplinary aspect [of teaching and] not being pigeonholed into one field."

Davies followed a path from high school to college that exposed him to several different fields until he narrowed down his choice to the new branch known as cognitive science. "In high school, I liked philosophy, so I majored in philosophy in college. During my senior year, I wasn't sure what I wanted to do so I was talking to the department chair. He asked if I had heard about cognitive science and gave me a book about it. It was so enthralling that I got an early job through Los Alamos National Lab, and while in grad school, I took courses in the philosophy, psychology, and cognitive science departments. I attended Georgia Tech for psychology, but they were not as friendly to computer modeling of the human mind as I would have liked."

Davies admitted it was difficult finding his first job given how new cognitive science was at the time, but over the last few years the field has grown. Cognitive science is made up of several different disciplines in which you can specialize. "Upon graduation, your career options go in two directions. There's the human-computer interaction work in non-academic jobs such as educational technology—creating software to help education. Human-computer interaction work means human testing and interface design. Microsoft, for example, has a huge research department to make sure their programs are useable and intuitive to the consumer. Adobe does the same thing. It's pretty easy to get a job in these areas, especially since they are growing so rapidly.

"Human factors, a related field, is less about computers and more about objects. Human factors might deal with things like how levers work in a cockpit, whereas human-computer interaction might mean designing the next generation of smart homes."

In addition to having taught at Ontario's Queen's University in Kingston, Davies was under a two-year contract for research. To him, being able to do both has it rewards. "Being an academic scientist is one of the best jobs in the world. You have tenure, a pension, flexible hours, and lots of vacation [time]," he noted.

Pure research is something many companies also engage in through their research and development departments. For example, Terry M. Turpin, senior vice president and chief scientist at Essex Corporation, a technology company, took Essex's optical processing work and studied using light waves to process information. If successful, Turpin's research may lead to a revolutionary leap in AI processing capability.

CHAPTER [5]

Cutting Edge Careers
Cutting Edge Careers
Careers

Cutting Edge Careers
Hot Cutting Edge Careers

# The Next Decade

Artificial Intelligence may be half a century old, but it is not a mature or aging field. With every new discovery in science or technology, researchers and scientists find fresh ways to apply computer technology to the discovery. AI will continue to find its way into every facet of life around the globe, attempting to make things more efficient for mankind.

*SmartMoney* magazine named AI careers in a group of "the Next Hot Jobs" in 2002, saying, "Artificial Intelligence used to be the stuff of sci-fi novels. Now it has spread from androids into all sorts of everyday fields, each of which is booming. Smart homes. Airport surveillance. Voice-recognition software. ATMs."

This mobile robot, playfully named the "Afghan Xplorer," was created at the Massachusetts Institute of Technology (MIT) to record data for reporters in hostile environments such as war zones.

Joanna Alexander, co-CEO of Seattle video game producer Zombie, said demand for more AI programmers in her industry alone will be boundless. "You have to build in a personality, responses, and realistic behavior for any characters you encounter," she said. "And games are only going to become more complex and more realistic."

Salaries in AI jobs typically start at $50,000 and climb to $70,000 to $80,000 after a few years. In most cases, applicants should have a four-year degree in either computer science with an AI specialty, or in mechanical or electrical engineering with a focus on robotics. Students now studying AI in college will find jobs undreamed of during their freshmen year. With more and more corporations devoting time and money to research, the job horizon is said to be exceptionally bright and promising.

"The future will involve many things, including machine learning. As a technique, this is probably the technique that has the most diverse array of applications. As you start thinking of careers, having a good background in machine learning will help you as you look at different careers," Google's Dr. Daniel Clancy said. "AI is becoming commonplace within almost all industries, from data mining to Amazon. The space companies like GE and Lockheed-Martin will use AI as a piece of the puzzle."

Dr. Clancy encourages students to consider a full range of AI applications, however, because it works with many other parallel systems. "Students need to understand a set of techniques to place AI in a proper context," he said. "They need to look at *solving* hard problems as opposed to being fixated with a particular *approach* to solving problems."

## Unparalleled Growth Rate

Microsoft's Eric Horvitz, who doubles as AAAI's president, takes a big-picture view of the field. Even after fifty years, he is convinced AI is still in its infancy. "I think we're just at the early days of computer science and the influence it'll have on the world," Horvitz said. "It's a very big growth area for careers. People also ask about AI: 'Will I lose my job?' There will be many jobs generated with people helping to create those machines that will shift the way things are done, bringing things to bear using intelligent reasoning and applications of various kinds.

"It's an interesting area, a high-impact area, and we're in the early days of it. I'm taking the long view. I'd say we're still flying canvass planes (as did the Wright Brothers) and in a shorter time than people realize, we'll have jumbo jets and fighters."

The cutting-edge career future in AI has tremendous possibilities. To Horvitz, the appeal of AI remains how it strives to understand the very things that make people human. He told the *New York Times* in 2006, "There's definitely been a palpable upswing in methods, competence and boldness. At conferences you are hearing the phrase 'human-level AI,' and people are saying that without blushing. AI is kind of the ultimate science because you're studying the science of self, the science of intelligence and the mind. You can actually bring together deep questions of the philosophical mind, with challenging problems in mathematics, and bring the results to real-world problems. The study of human psychology . . . how can we build systems that can take insights from the way people's minds work, how do you build systems that let people work together, collaboratively with computers, complementing people's skills.

"I tell my people that the number-one task, the number-one goal, is to extend the state of the art. Forget about Microsoft; think five to ten years out, if not more. Two, if the stuff you're doing happens to have relevance to Microsoft products sooner, even better. We have an open publication model, allowing researchers to publish what they like. They're free to work and publish. Microsoft attracts a certain kind of person who has a hankering for creating a positive value for large numbers of people."

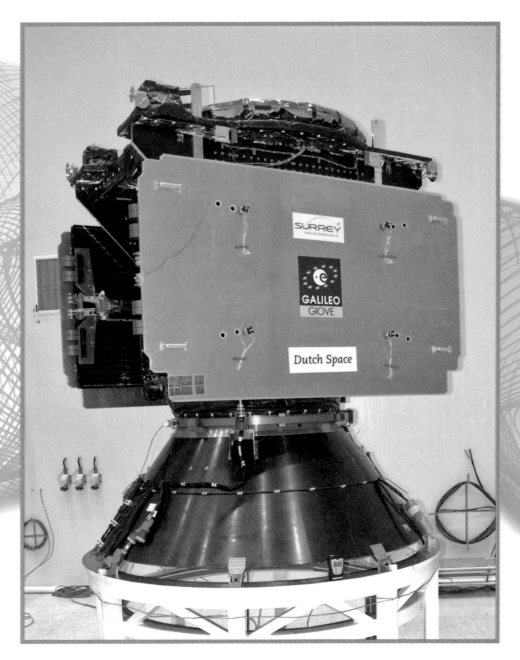

The European Space Agency (ESA) launched Europe's global navigation satellite system, *Galileo*, in 2005 as a rival to the United States' Global Positioning System (GPS).

# Everything Will Be Wired

Google's Dr. Francis said, "The future for AI careers is very bright. You look at the world 100 years ago and nothing had nerves except a few telegraph wires. Every object was 'dead' [unwired]. You look at the world a century from now and everything will be wired. We won't be having a phone to hold a conversation. Maybe the very paint on the walls will be the projection screen, and simply writing notes on the desktop will be transmittable because the desk will be a wired object. That potential future is going to present far more information to the world than a human can process. Without help, it'll be unmanageable."

According to Dr. Francis, computers and machines will be a great deal "smarter" about how they present information. The great uses and applications of AI will be necessary to manage information so that the machines may respond to people in ways that are more useful and efficient. To do that, computer scientists and AI experts need to model human response to everything from the way we perceive the world to how to spend our discretionary time. "Artificial intelligence will be creating machines that take the full pipeline of information that the world generates, that can understand language as well as humans, that can summarize what they know into useful information, and that can make decisions that humans will think will make sense," Dr. Francis said.

The most visible solution to human problems will be robots, as seen with Honda's ASIMO (named after Isaac Asimov), but the applications will seep into almost every mechanical device. Additionally, computer scientist and author Ray Kurzweil wrote, "Non-biological intelligence will match the capabilities of human intelligence by 2029. And in the 2030s, we will merge with this technology by sending intelligent nanobots [micro robots] into our brains through the capillaries." In his 2006 book, *The Singularity Is Near*, Kurzweil

The hand of Mark W. Tilden, robobiologist at the Los Alamos National Laboratory in New Mexico, displays robot components that are capable of working in hazardous environments.

went so far as to predict that human genetics, artificial intelligence, and nanotechnology will converge by 2045. To get there, people will need to apply their creativity in careers that can only be found on the cutting edge.

# GLOSSARY

**agent**  A program that continuously performs tasks, adapting and learning an individual's needs.

**algorithm**  A sequence of rules and instructions that describes a procedure to solve a problem. A computer program expresses one or more algorithms in a manner understandable by a computer.

**computer**  A machine that implements an algorithm (aka computer program) and related data. A computer transforms data according to the specifications of an algorithm.

**digital**  Varying in discrete steps. The use of combinations of bits to represent data in computation.

**dystopia**  A society characterized by oppression, human strife, and misery; opposite meaning of utopia.

**expert systems**  These apply reasoning capabilities to reach a conclusion. An expert system can process large amounts of known information and provide conclusions based on them.

**fuzzy logic**  This is a variation of Boolean logic designed to handle the concept of values between "completely true" and "completely false." The addition of fuzzy logic made expert systems more adept at tasks such as pattern recognition and forecasting the behavior of the stock market.

**nanotechnology**  A body of technology in which products and other objects are created through the manipulation of atoms and molecules.

neural network A form of multiprocessor computer system with basic processing elements, a high degree of interconnection, simple messages, and adaptive interaction between elements.

punch card A rectangular card that typically records up to eighty characters of data in a binary coded format as a pattern of holes punched in it.

robot A programmable device, linked to a computer, consisting of mechanical manipulators and sensors. A robot may perform a physical task normally done by human beings, possibly with greater speed, strength, and/or precision.

software Information and knowledge used to perform useful functions by computers and computerized devices. Includes computer programs and their data, but more generally also includes such knowledge products as books, music, pictures, movies, and videos.

technology An evolving process of tool creation to shape and control the environment. Technology goes beyond the mere fashioning and using of tools. It involves a record of tool making and a progression in the sophistication of tools. It requires invention and is itself a continuation of evolution by other means. The "genetic code" of the evolutionary process of technology is the knowledge base maintained by the tool-making species.

virtual reality A simulated environment in which you can immerse yourself. A virtual reality environment provides a convincing replacement for the visual and auditory senses.

Zeitgeist The spirit of the time; the outlook of a period.

# FOR MORE INFORMATION

American Association for Artificial Intelligence
445 Burgess Drive, Suite 100
Menlo Park, CA 94025
(650) 328-3123
Web site: http://www.aaai.org

Computer History Museum
1401 N. Shoreline Boulevard
Mountain View, CA 94043
(650) 810-1010
Web site: http://www.computerhistory.org

Google Headquarters
1600 Amphitheatre Parkway
Mountain View, CA 94043
Web site: http://www.google.com/jobs/students.html

Institute of Electrical and Electronics Engineers Computer Society
1730 Massachusetts Avenue NW
Washington, DC 20036-1992
(202) 371-0101
Web site: http://www.computer.org

National Workforce Center for Emerging Technologies
3000 Landerholm Circle SE

Bellevue, WA 98007
(425) 564-4215
Web site: http://www.nwcet.org

The Society for the Study of Artificial Intelligence and the Simulation
of Behaviour
School of Science and Technology, University of Sussex
Falmer, Brighton, BN1 9QH
England
Web site: http://www.aisb.org.uk

## Web Sites

Due to the changing nature of Internet links, Rosen Publishing has
developed an online list of Web sites related to the subject of this
book. This site is updated regularly. Please use this link to access
the list:

http://www.rosenlinks.com/cec/arin

# FOR FURTHER READING

Asimov, Isaac. *I Robot*. New York, NY: Bantam Spectra, 1950.

Backlund, Mat (sic). *Programming AI by Example*. Plano, TX: Woodware Publishing, 2004.

Boden, Margaret A. *The Philosophy of Artificial Intelligence*. Oxford, England: Oxford University Press, 1990.

Gaudette, Pat. *Sparky the Aibo: Robot Dogs & Other Robotic Pets*. Roanoke, VI: Home & Leisure Publishing, 2002.

Gerrold, David. *When Harley Was One*. New York, NY: Bantam Spectra, 1972.

Fung, John David. *Artificial Intelligence for Computer Games: An Introduction*. New York, NY: Peters Corp., 2004.

Heinlein, Robert A. *The Moon Is a Harsh Mistress*. New York, NY: Orb Books, 1966.

Hogan, James P. *Mind Matters*. New York, NY: DelRey Books, 1997.

Hsu, Feng-Hsiung. *Behind Deep Blue: Building the Computer that Defeated the World Chess Champion*. Princeton, NJ: Princeton University Press, 2004.

Jackson, Philip C. *Introduction to Artificial Intelligence*, 2nd enlarged ed. New York, NY: Dover Books, 1985.

Leavitt, David. *The Man Who Knew Too Much: Alan Turning and the Invention of the Computer*. New York, NY: W. W. Norton, 2005.

McCorduck, Pamela. *Machines Who Think*. London, England: A. K. Peters Limited, 2004.

Minsky, Marvin. *Society of Mind*. New York, NY: Simon & Schuster, 1998.

Rabin, Steve. *AI Game Programming Wisdom*. Revere, MA: Charles River Media, 2002.

Russel, Stuart J., and Peter Norvig. *Artificial Intelligence: A Modern Approach*. New York, NY: Prentice Hall, 2002.

Scientific American. *Understanding Artificial Intelligence*. New York, NY: Warner Books, 2002.

# BIBLIOGRAPHY

Brooks, Rodney A. *Flesh and Machine.* New York, NY: Pantheon Books, 2002.

Butterman, Eric, and Travis C. Daub. "Artificial Intelligence Has Long Been Considered an Interesting Plot Device for Science Fiction Stories—but Not Much More." Graduating Engineer Online. Retrieved February 27, 2006 (http://www.graduatingengineer. com/articles/feature/04-09-01a.html).

*Career Information Center*, 8th edition. New York, NY: MacMillan Reference, 2002.

Caudill, Maureen. *In Our Image.* Oxford, England: Oxford University Press, 1992.

Engleberger, Joseph F. *Robotics in Service.* Cambridge, MA: MIT Press, 1989.

Goldstein, Alan H. "I, Nanobot." Salon.com. Retrieved March 16, 2006 (http://www.salon.com/tech/feature/2006/03/09/ nanobiobot/print.html).

Hampshire, Nick. "Artificial Intelligence: Working Backwards from HAL." ZDNet UK. Retrieved March 16, 2006 (http://insight.zdnet. co.uk/hardware/emergingtech/0,39020439,39259512,00.htm).

Hogan, James P. *Mind Matters.* New York, NY: DelRey Books, 1997.

Koch, Geoff. "Artificial Intelligence Pioneer Ponders Differences Between Computers and Humans." Stanford Report. Retrieved February 27, 2006 (http://news-service.stanford.edu/news/ 2003/october29/nilsson-1029.html).

Kurzweil, Ray. *The Age of Spiritual Machines*. New York, NY: Viking, 1999.

Morkes, Andrew, ed. *The Encyclopedia of Careers and Vocational Guidance*, 12th edition. Chicago, IL: Ferguson Publishing Company, 2003.

Moustris, George. "AI as a Career." About.com. Retrieved February 27, 2006 (http://experts.about.com/q/Artificial-Intelligence-2506/AI-Career.htm).

Partridge, Derek. *Artificial Intelligence and Software Engineering*. Chicago, IL: Glenlake Publishing Company, Ltd., 1998.

Roan, Shari. "Science Quickens Its Steps." *Los Angeles Times*. Retrieved March 16, 2006 (http://www.latimes.com/la-he-amputee9mar09,0,236454.story).

Rogoff, Kenneth. "Artificial Intelligence and Globalization." DailyTimes.com. Retrieved March 16, 2006 (http://www.dailytimes.com.pk/default.asp?page=2006%5C03%5C05%5Cstory_5-3-2006_pg5_26).

Shabelman, David. "The Driving Force Behind Yahoo Research." CNet News. Retrieved March 16, 2006 (http://news.com.com/The+driving+force+behind+Yahoo+Research/2100-1024_3-6044575.html).

Sloman, Aaron. "What Is Artificial Intelligence?" University of Birmingham, School of Computer Sciences. Retrieved February 27, 2006 (http://www.cs.bham.ac.uk/~axs/misc/aiforschools.html).

U.S. Department of Labor. *Occupational Outlook Handbook, 2006–07 Edition*. Washington, DC.

# INDEX

## About the Author

Robert Greenberger is a writer with a wide range of credits, including more than a dozen educational, nonfiction titles for young adults. He has also written for DC Comics, Marvel Comics, sci-fi.com, and *Weekly World News*, where he spends his days as Production Manager. Additionally, he has written original science fiction and fantasy stories for young people and adults. Greenberger lives in Connecticut.

## Photo Credits

Cover (top) © Andrei Tchernov/www.istockphoto.com; cover (bottom), pp. 20, 21 © MarioTama/Getty Images; pp. 4–5 Bruce Rolff/Shutterstock.com; pp. 8, 10–11 © Bettmann/Corbis; p. 12 © Michael Poche/AP/Wide World Photos; p. 13 © Rick Friedman/Corbis; p. 17 © Matt Houston/AP/Wide World Photos; p. 18 © Mark Cowan/AP/Wide World Photos; p. 24 © www.civ3.com; p. 26 © David McNew/Getty Images; p. 27 © University of Pennsylvania/AP/Wide World Photos; p. 31 © Tim Larson/AP/Wide World Photos; p. 33 © NASA Headquarters–Greatest Images of NASA (NASA-HQ-GRIN); p. 35 © www.amazon.com; p. 37 © Justin Sullivan/Getty Images; p. 41 © Suchat Pederson/AP/Wide World Photos; p. 43 © Steve Shelton/AP/Wide World Photos; p. 48 © MIT Media Lab/Getty Images; p. 51 © Stringer/AFP/Getty Images; p. 53 © Joe Marquette/AP/Wide World Photos.

Editor: Joann Jovinelly; Series Designer: Evelyn Horovicz
Photo Researcher: Hillary Arnold